The Science of a Spring

John Stringer

WAYLAND

Science World

Other titles in the series:

The Science of
Gravity

The Science of a
Light Bulb

The Science of
Noise

Picture acknowledgements
Wayland Publishers would like to thank the following for allowing their pictures to be reproduced in this book:
Action-Plus/Steve Bardens 7; Bubbles/Pauline Cutler *cover* [inset middle], 6; Martyn F. Chillmaid 4 (bottom);
Eye Ubiquitous/NASA 19 (bottom), /Paul Seheult 25 (bottom); Getty Images/Dan Bosler 26, /Chuck Davis 21,
/Mark Harwood *title page*, /Renee Lynn *cover* [main], 27, /World Perspectives 14; Robert Harding 24 (bottom),
/Eric Sanford 9; Paul Humphrey/Discovery Books 15 (bottom); Impact/Garaini Lewis 10; Popperphoto 22, /Bob
Thomas 8 (top); Science Photo Library 19 (top), /Jerrican Aurel 24 (top), /Sheila Terry 28; /Jerome Yeats 8
(middle); Trip/H. Rogers *contents page*; John Walmsley 18; Wayland Picture Library *cover* [inset top], 4 (top and
middle), 8 (bottom) 12, 15 (top), 17, 25 (top and middle).

The chapter logo and illustrations on pages 5, 7, 13, 16, 20, 23, 28 and 29 are by Peter Bull.
The illustrations on page 11 are by Rudi Vizi.

Editor: Carron Brown
Consultant: Anne Goldsworthy
Series design: Lisa Nutt
Designer: Mark Whitchurch
Production controller: Carol Stevens

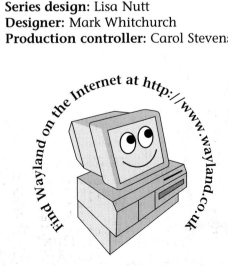

Find Wayland on the Internet at http://www.wayland.co.uk

First published in 1999 by Wayland Publishers Ltd,
61 Western Road, Hove, East Sussex BN3 1JD

British Library in Cataloguing Data
Stringer, John
  The Science of a Spring. – (Science World)
  1. Springs (Mechanism) – Juvenile literature
  2. Force and energy – Juvenile literature
  I. Title
  621.8'24

ISBN 0 7502 2401 0

Contents

Types of spring

Think about springs. What do you know about them? Springs are found in many unexpected places.

There are probably springs in your bed, and springs in your clock. ▼

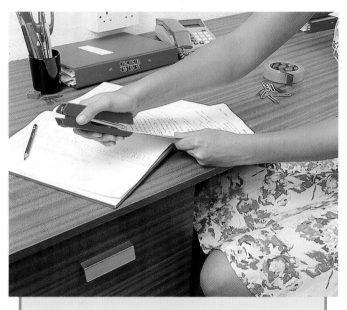

▲ There are springs in a stapler. Paper clips are also types of springs.

There is even a spring on the ▶ shutter of each floppy disc!

In fact, you are probably surrounded by springs.

How does a stapler work?

If you look inside a stapler, you will see two types of springs: a flat leaf spring lifts the arm back after you have stapled something; and a long coil spring pushes the next staple into place.

This leaf spring pushes open the stapler after stapling.

This coil spring pushes the next staple forward.

Shapes of springs

There are two main types of springs: leaf springs and coil springs. Leaf springs are flat pieces of metal, and coil springs are coiled pieces of metal.

Springs that squash and bend

When you push some springs, you squeeze them or bend them and they change shape. Springs that are squashed or bent always try to go back to their original shape.

What happens when you stand on a pogo stick?

A pogo stick has a coiled spring at the bottom. When you jump on a pogo stick, the spring is squashed by your weight. When it's squashed, the spring jumps back into its original shape and bounces you into the air.

Springs that bend are called leaf springs. Leaf springs bend and then return to how they were. You can see them clearly on car trailers and some caravans.

The leaf spring on this trailer ▶ is squashed when the trailer is loaded.

leaf spring

Beds and chairs use springs that squash so that you can get comfortable. Cars and other vehicles and some mountain bikes use coiled springs near the wheels so that you are comfortable when travelling over bumpy surfaces.

This mountain bike ▶ has springs attached to its frame near the wheels. These soften the bumps for the rider and make the journey more enjoyable.

Springs that stretch

Some springs can be stretched. Like springs that squash, springs that are stretched try to get back to their original shape.

There are many stretchy springs around you. They are in baby bouncers and the straps that hold objects on to your bike. They are used in gymnasium equipment, such as rowing machines. They are even in your clothes. Without the stretchy material in the waistband, your pants would fall down!

▲ This baby bouncer has a springy metal frame. It bends, gently bouncing the baby.

This rowing machine has long coil springs ▶ on the foot blocks. When you push, you stretch them. When you relax, the springs pull the blocks back.

The stretchy clothes on this gymnast move ▼ with her body. She even has a stretchy hair band to hold back her hair.

If you were to leap from a crane with a bungee rope tied to your ankles, the bungee rope stretches. As it stretches, the rope slows you down more and more, and stops you hitting the ground. The bungee rope is stretched most as you reach the end of your fall; then it begins pulling you back.

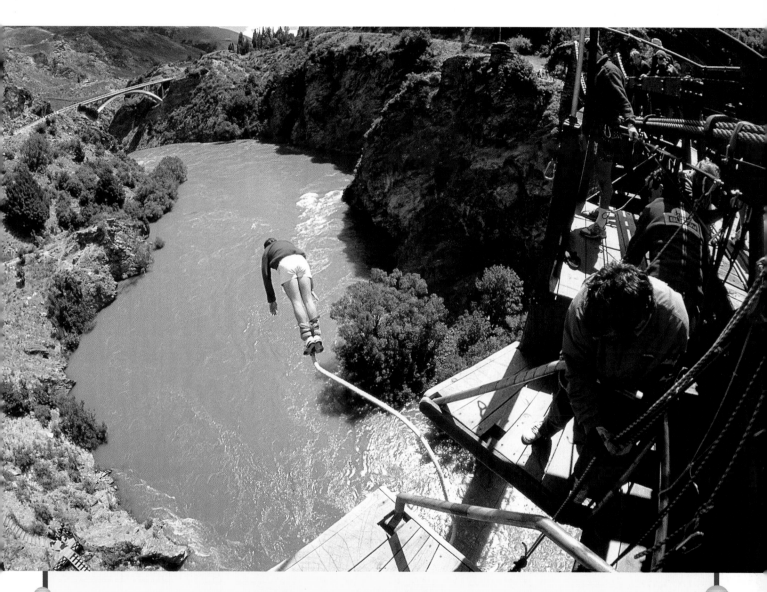

How long does a bungee rope stretch?

The world's record bungee jump was from a helicopter. The bungee rope stretched from 250 m long to over 600 m long.

Forces and springs

Springs work because of forces. To understand how springs work, we need to learn about these forces. A force is a push or a pull. The best way to show how forces work is to use pictures. We can show the directions of the forces at work using arrows. We can also show the size of the force – the longer the arrow, the stronger the force.

When forces are balanced

When there is no movement, forces are still at work but they are balanced.

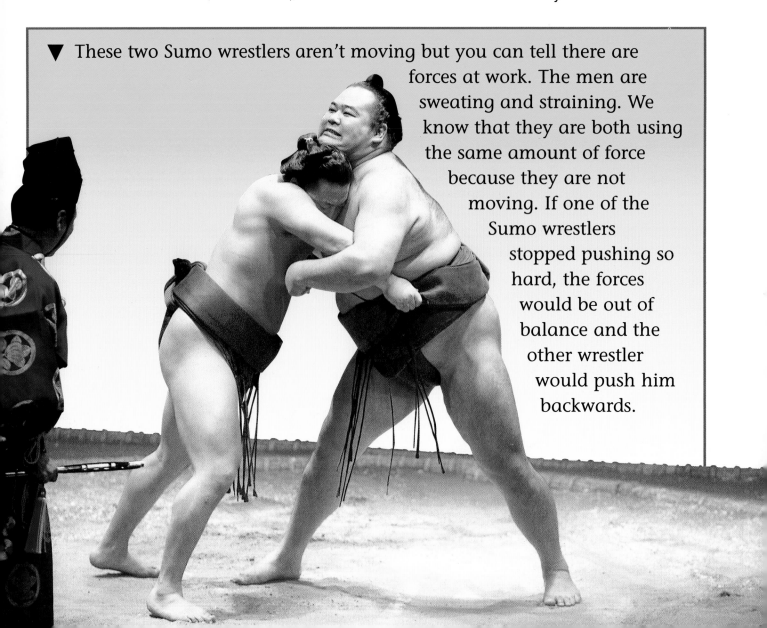

▼ These two Sumo wrestlers aren't moving but you can tell there are forces at work. The men are sweating and straining. We know that they are both using the same amount of force because they are not moving. If one of the Sumo wrestlers stopped pushing so hard, the forces would be out of balance and the other wrestler would push him backwards.

These two tug-of-war teams aren't moving so the forces must be balanced. Both teams are using the same amount of pulling force. If any more people joined the team on the right, the forces would be unbalanced as the right team's pull would be stronger.

Once the forces become unbalanced, the team with the stronger pull can win by pulling the team with the weaker pull over a line between them.

It's not so easy to show the ▶ forces acting on this football. There are two forces at work: a pulling force called gravity and a pushing force. Gravity is pulling the ball down towards the centre of the Earth. So why doesn't the ball go down? Something is stopping it. The ground is pushing back on the ball. Gravity and the push of the ground are in balance. The ball stays where it is!

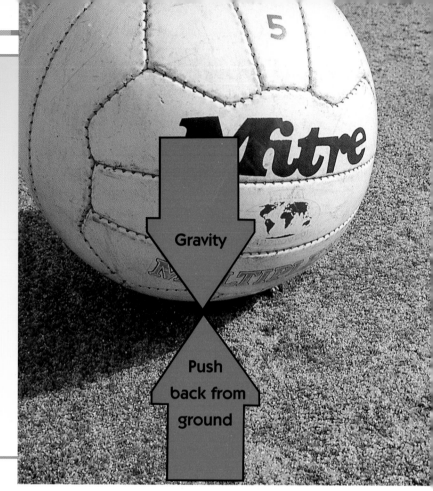

A book on a table is being ▼ pulled down by gravity. The table is pushing back to keep the book where it is. The arrows show these forces.

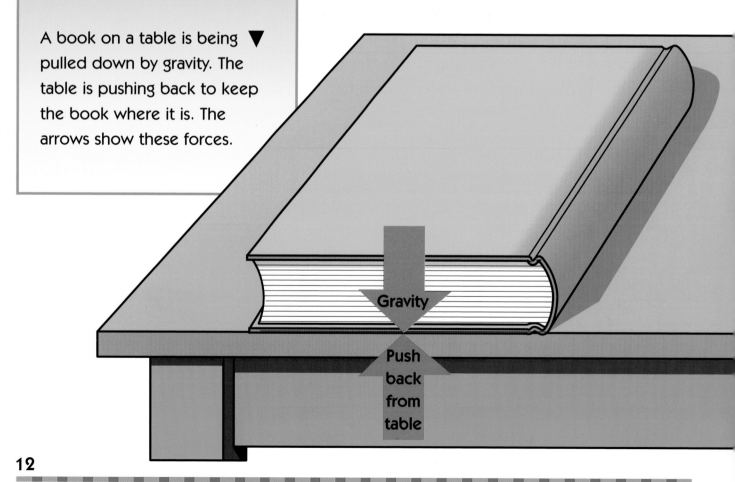

Are hard objects springy?

When you squeeze a hard object, such as a wooden table leg or a stone, its hard surface pushes back. It changes a little but it looks like it stays in much the same shape.

However, even hard surfaces, such as steel and glass, are slightly springy! If something pushes down on a hard surface, it acts a bit like a very stiff trampoline. Objects bounce when they fall and hit something. They also change shape a tiny bit and spring back into shape.

▼ Glass marbles bounce because they change shape a tiny bit as they hit the floor.

1. A marble falls to the floor.

2. As it hits the floor it changes shape a little – it goes flatter at the bottom.

3. As it springs back into shape, it bounces up again.

4. The marble finally settles on the floor in its original shape.

The faster an object can spring back into shape, the higher it will bounce. Power balls made of springy plastic get their shape back very quickly and bounce very high.

When forces are unbalanced

Sometimes when forces are unbalanced, there is movement. A rocket blasting off from Cape Kennedy, USA is being held back by the downward pull of gravity. But as gravity is a weaker force than the tremendous upward force of the rocket engines, the forces are unbalanced and so the rocket climbs into the sky.

This rocket will use unbalanced forces to blast out of the Earth's atmosphere. ▼

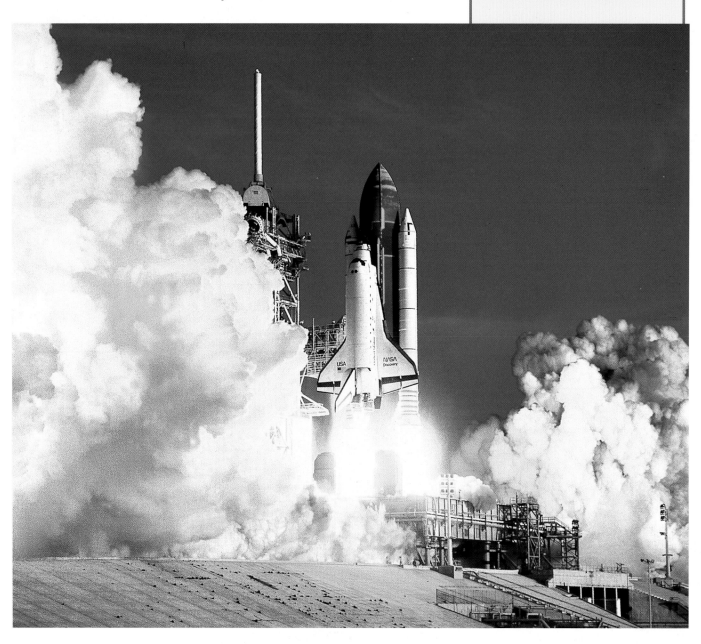

Sometimes, when forces are unbalanced, objects change shape.

Try squeezing a block of wood or ▶ metal – these are substances that push back hard.

◀ When you squeeze some plasticine, the plasticine pushes back but not enough to stop it changing shape. If the plasticine pushed back as hard as you squeezed, you would hardly change its shape at all.

When you squeeze or stretch a spring, the forces are unbalanced. The spring changes shape. But when you stop squeezing or stretching, your force stops acting and the spring's force jumps it back to shape.

▲ When a spring stays in the same shape, the forces will be balanced. You may feel the spring pushing into you.

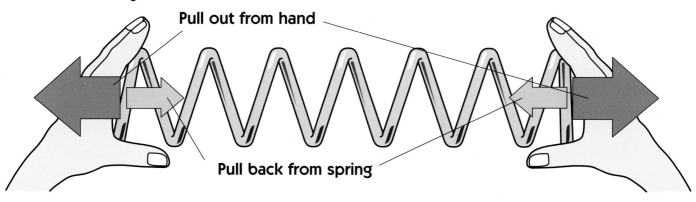

Pull out from hand

Pull back from spring

▲ When you stretch a spring, you are using a stronger pulling force than the pull back from the spring.

Push out from hand

Push out from spring

◀ When you squash a spring, you are using a stronger pushing force than the pull back from the spring.

The spring returns to ▶ its original shape if you release it.

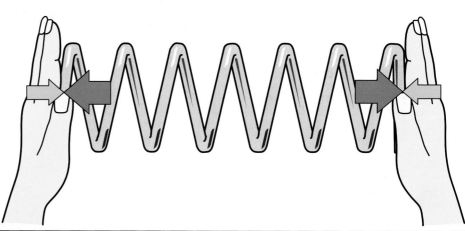

Will a spring stretch forever?

A spring will not stretch forever. A spring reaches the point where it will no longer stretch. Scientists call this point the elastic limit.

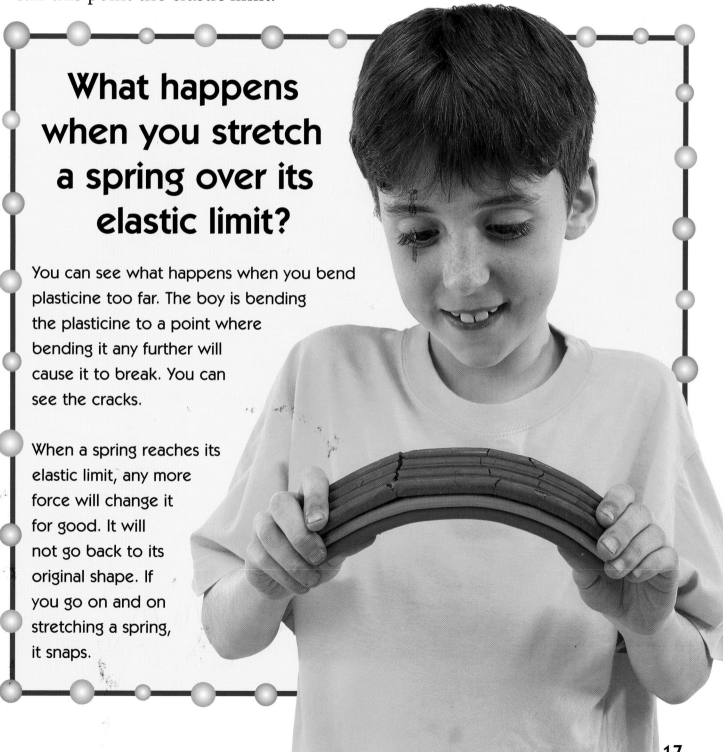

What happens when you stretch a spring over its elastic limit?

You can see what happens when you bend plasticine too far. The boy is bending the plasticine to a point where bending it any further will cause it to break. You can see the cracks.

When a spring reaches its elastic limit, any more force will change it for good. It will not go back to its original shape. If you go on and on stretching a spring, it snaps.

Weight and the Earth's pull

The Earth pulls on every object. The amount of this pull is called the object's weight.

How do we measure a pull force?

A newton meter measures the size of a pull force. It has a spring inside so it can measure the pull on an object. The Earth pulls down on the object and the object pulls on the spring. The stretched spring moves a pointer which shows how much the object weighs.

A newton meter can also measure how much pull force is needed to pull an object along a surface. When you pull an object along with a newton meter, you are measuring the force needed to move it. Forces are measured in newtons.

Sir Isaac Newton

Newtons are named after Sir Isaac Newton, an English scientist who lived between 1642–1727. One famous story tells of how he watched an apple fall to the ground. This started him thinking about the force of gravity and why everything falls down to the ground, not sideways or up.

A 1 kg bag of sugar is pulled down towards the Earth with a force of 10 newtons. The Earth pulls down on a mass of 100g with a force of about 1 newton. One newton is about equal to the weight of a medium-sized apple.

The Earth's pull ▶ gives us weight. Without it, we would float into space.

Springs all around us

We know that springs work because of forces, and that they can be bent, squashed or stretched. Would you recognize the springs in use around you?

Are you sitting comfortably?

When you sit on a soft chair or lie on a bed, you are squeezing some springs. As you first sit down, the forces are unbalanced. Your weight is greater than the push back from the springs. The springs get shorter until they can't be squashed any more. The forces have become balanced because the springs push back on you as hard as you are pushing down on them. You are sitting comfortably. When you stand up, the springs return to their original size.

◀ You can see how the springs are supporting the girl's weight in the chair to help her sit in comfort.

Some chairs and beds work by stretching springs, rather than squashing them. There are elastic bands or springs across the frames, which stretch when you sit down.

Can we stop buildings cracking in earthquakes?

In parts of the world that have earthquakes, tall buildings are built on springs. The springs absorb the force of the earthquake and prevent a building breaking up (as in this picture) and falling down.

What absorbs the bumps?

You may travel in a car, a bus or a train. If it had no springs, you would be jarred by every bump. Your journey would be very uncomfortable; and you would be very sore at the end of it!

▲ This vehicle is designed with springs and dampers that will make even the most bumpy journey comfortable.

The coil springs on a car take up the force of the bumps. The jolts cannot be felt as much in the car. But springs alone would make the car bounce. So cars have dampers which slow down the movement of the springs and stop you bouncing up and down!

Coil springs on cars are between the axles and the rest of the car. When the car is loaded, the springs are squashed. They smooth out the bumps. Dampers stop the car bouncing.

The springs are between the wheel axles and the rest of the car.

The coil spring is slightly squashed on a flat road.

The coil spring is squashed as the car bounces over the bumps.

Springing back into shape

There are many objects that use springs that spring back into shape. Springy objects can give us a lot of fun.

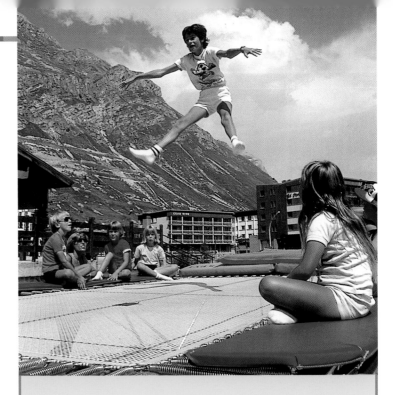

▼ When you pull back on a bow and arrow, you are using a spring. The pulling force of your arm changes the shape of the bow, which slowly bends like a big leaf spring. When you let go, the arrow is fired as the bow springs back into its original shape.

▲ When you jump on a trampoline, it acts like a big spring, springing back into shape and bouncing you into the air.

When you wind up a clock or mechanical watch, you are winding up a spring. As it gradually unwinds, it will turn the hands of the clock and tell you the time.

◀ This clock has a key at the back that you can turn to wind up the spring inside.

Clockwork toys were ▶ very popular before electric motors and batteries became cheaper. The springs inside them made parts move.

▼ The inside of a wind-up clock looks like this. You can see a long metal ribbon coiled tight where a key has turned to wind it. It is made to unwind slowly on to the round metal cylinder, turning all the gears to make the clock work.

Your springy body

Your body is full of springs and stretchy bits. If it wasn't, you would have to move round like a robot. You wouldn't be able to jump, and you could not absorb the shock of landing.

▲ When you run, your foot hits the ground with a force of two or three times your body weight. If you ran in a marathon, your foot would be hitting the ground like this 25,000 times. Your ankles and knees would be damaged without some sort of body springs.

Do animals have springs?

Animals need springy parts inside them too. Tigers need to be able to run and pounce to catch food.

A tiger's legs are the most powerful parts of its body. It relies on a sharp burst of speed and a strong pounce to kill its prey. The 'springs' in a tiger's legs cushion the force of its pounce.

There are bags of fluid in your joints that act like springs, absorbing some of this shock. However, they cannot stand endless pounding. This is why you should wear cushioned springy shoes when playing sports. Training shoes are designed to absorb forces.

Springs in locks

All locks work using springs, from
padlocks to your front door lock.

1. Coiled springs hold down
metal pins that can only be
moved by the correct key.

2. The turning key keeps
a bolt in place in the door.

3. This coiled spring pushes the
bolt, and keeps the door locked.

The lock on your front door contains a lot of tiny
springs. They are above a row of metal pins. Only
the pattern of your door key will push the springs
back and line the pins up so that the lock will
turn.

As the lock turns, it pulls in the bolt locking the door to the wall. The door opens. When you let go of your key, another spring pushes the bolt back.

2. These springs push down the pins. If the key fits the pins, the key will turn.

3. The turning key twists this cam and pulls back the bolt.

1. You turn the key.

4. When you let the key go, this spring pushes the bolt back, ready to lock the door again.

Glossary

Axles The poles on which a wheel turns: for example, in a vehicle.

Balanced forces When two forces are equal and act in opposition to each other.

Cam A cam is a wheel that turns round and round movement into up and down.

Clockwork A machine with a coil spring which you wind up.

Coil spring This spring is coiled, and can be pushed and pulled.

Damper On a car, a tube filled with fluid that stops the springs bouncing too much. Dampers are also called shock absorbers.

Elastic Something that is able to go back to its original shape or length after being stretched or squashed.

Elastic limit A spring at its elastic limit will not stretch any further and go back to its original shape. Any more force will change its shape for good.

Forces Pushes or pulls between objects.

Gravity This force is the Earth's pull on everything. Every object has a force of gravity, but the Earth's is by far the largest.

Leaf springs Flat springs that bend when pushed or pulled.

Mass The amount of matter in an object.

newton (N) The unit we use to measure force, named after Sir Isaac Newton.

Unbalanced forces When two forces are unequal, and force is greater than the other.

Weight Weight is a force. An object's weight is the pull of the Earth on it. The measure of its weight depends on its mass.

Further Information

Books to read

Clocks, Scales and Movement (*Science Workshop* series) by Peter Robson (Watts, 1995)

Earth (*Connections!* series) by Caroline Grimshaw (Two-Can, 1995)

Earth and Beyond (*Essential Science Cards*) by John Stringer and Malcolm Ward (Channel 4 Learning, 1999)

Forces and Movement (*Straightforward Science* series) by Peter Riley (Watts, 1998)

The Science of Gravity by John Stringer (Wayland, 1999)

Websites to visit

www.nmsi.ac.uk/welcome.html
This is the home page of the Science Museum.

www.askeric.org/Projects/Newton
This site contains many interesting science lessons.

Places to visit

The Science Museum, Exhibition Road, South Kensington, London (Tel: 0171 938 8000) has a special locks exhibit where you can see how various locks work. You will also find many objects that work using springs.

Woolsthorpe Manor, Grantham, Lincolnshire (Tel: 01476 860338) is Sir Isaac Newton's home, where he made many of his discoveries.

MUSIC
• Compose a piece of music that describes the many movements of a spring in action.

GEOGRAPHY
• Investigate the areas of the world that need earthquake protection.

HISTORY
• Find out about the story of Sir Isaac Newton and his discoveries.
• Find out more about mechanical clocks and their history.

ART AND CRAFT
• Look at the patterns of different springs.

Spring
TOPIC WEB

DESIGN AND TECHNOLOGY
• Look at the designs of different locks and how they use springs.
• Look at pictures of different vehicles, and think about why they would need dampers and leaf springs.
• Investigate how buildings are protected from being damaged by earthquakes.

SCIENCE
• Explore pushes and pulls – look at how forces work.
• Investigate what objects around you contain springs and how they work.
• Explore balanced and unbalanced forces.

MATHS
• Measurement: e.g. newtons, weight, mass.

ENGLISH
• Write a poem based on the motion of springs: i.e. bouncing on a trampoline; doing a bungee jump.

Index

Numbers in **bold** refer to pictures as well as text.